# YOU'RE BEING DUPED

## Fake News on Social Media

Jennifer Peters

**Enslow Publishing**
101 W. 23rd Street
Suite 240
New York, NY 10011
USA

enslow.com

Published in 2020 by Enslow Publishing, LLC
101 W. 23rd Street, Suite 240, New York, NY 10011

**Library of Congress Cataloging-in-Publication Data**

Names: Peters, Jennifer.
Title: You're being duped : fake news on social media / Jennifer Peters.
Description: New York : Enslow Publishing, 2020. | Series: Social media
  smarts | Includes bibliographical references and index. | Audience: Grade 5-8.
Identifiers: LCCN 2018055036| ISBN 9781978507753 (library bound) | ISBN
  9781978507746 (pbk.)
Subjects: LCSH: Media literacy—Juvenile literature. | Fake news—Juvenile
  literature. | Social media—Juvenile literature.
Classification: LCC P96.M4 P48 2019 | DDC 302.23/1—dc23
LC record available at https://lccn.loc.gov/2018055036

Printed in the United States of America

**To Our Readers:** We have done our best to make sure all website addresses in this book were active and appropriate when we went to press. However, the author and the publisher have no control over and assume no liability for the material available on those websites or on any websites they may link to. Any comments or suggestions can be sent by email to customerservice@enslow.com.

# Contents

# Introduction

Today, you can learn about anything you want online. It's easier than ever to find any bit of information that piques your interest, from biographical data about your favorite celebrities to how-to guides on making slime to tips on acing your upcoming math test. You can also read the news and keep up with what's happening in the world around you. But with so much information out there, how do you know if what you're reading is even worth your time—or if it's real?

Social media has made it incredibly simple to share what you see online with your friends, family—even complete strangers. And while most of the people sharing information with you mean the best, not all of them are going to know if they're sharing bad information or fake news. That's because every link shared on social media looks essentially the same. If you post a story to Facebook about a new panda being born at the zoo, that post will look almost exactly like a post you share about a mass shooting. The pictures and text may be different, but they'll be given the same weight and the same style, and their links will look equally trustworthy.

On Twitter, it's also easy to share information. This means fake news can spread like wildfire. Anyone can create an account to share whatever information they want. They can even make accounts that look like those of people you know or trust. You may think you're reading a tweet posted by Taylor Swift, but it could be a very good fake. Or maybe you think you've found your community's newspaper online. That should

Mark Zuckerberg is the founder and CEO of Facebook, the largest social media platform in the world. Most people in your life probably have a Facebook account!

Taylor Swift is one of the most famous pop stars in the world, so lots of people pretend to be her online in order to fool others into reading and sharing their social media posts.

be simple enough, right? But that, too, could easily be faked. Twitter tries to make it easier to know who's posting by giving certain accounts blue checkmarks to prove users are who they say they are. But not every account that is legitimate gets such verification. Some accounts might even create a fake seal of approval to trick you.

There are many people looking to trick you online—people who want you to read fake news and share their false information so that you will fool other people with their fake stories. And telling the difference between the bad actors and the good isn't easy. It's even harder than telling a fake news story from a real one. But it's not impossible.

Before you can learn how to combat fake news, you have to understand what it is—and what it isn't. As you read the following chapters, you'll learn about what fake news is, how it spreads, how you can figure out if what you're reading is quality information, and how you can make sure you're part of the solution—not part of the problem.

# What Is Fake News?

**F**ake news gets a lot of play in the media when people are upset. Sometimes it can feel like everyone from politicians to average citizens uses the term "fake news" to mean anything they don't like or disagree with. But that's not really fake news. Instead, fake news is something far more sinister.

## The Dark Side of the Information Super Highway

Fake news has been around since the invention of the printing press. One of the earliest and most well-known fake news stories was published in 1835 and is known as the Great Moon Hoax.[1] The hoax included a series of news stories published in the *New York Sun* claiming that life had been discovered on the moon. But those stories were completely fake. The articles were intended to be satirical—fake stories meant to poke fun at writers who took their subjects too seriously. These stories pretended to have information about life on the moon, though no such information existed.

The Great Moon Hoax of 1835 was one of the original fake news stories. The articles convinced readers there was a civilization on the moon, though we know now that was not true.

Many people who read the *Sun* fell for the Great Moon Hoax. It was printed right there in their daily newspaper alongside other, factual, stories. Readers had no reason not to trust the stories about life on the moon. Why would they think the moon stories were false? The fact that they were printed in a newspaper added to the believability of the hoax. People had no reason to believe that someone would publish lies in a real printed newspaper.

While today's fake news has moved online, it's just as dangerous and people are just as likely to fall for the stories as they were nearly two hundred years ago. And that's by design.

Fake news is supposed to look real. The people who design the websites and write the fake stories go to great lengths to make sure that their false news articles look and sound as believable as genuine, quality news.[2] And creating such believable fake news is as easy as it's ever been, thanks to

**Newspapers rely on real editors and reporters to share factual, verified news about the world with their readers**

the internet. Fake news producers can build a website and a social media presence overnight. They can share their stories alongside trusted publishers and journalists. This ends up confusing readers.

That confusion is the goal of fake news. Fake news aims to spread misinformation and confuse the public by making it impossible to know which source can be believed, which story is true, and which reporters can be trusted.

By making all news suspect, fake news creators make their false stories more likely to spread. And they do this for a number of reasons. Some fake news creators want to sow

## Facing the Fact-Checks

Debunking fake news has become an important job in the past few years, and one of the original online fact-checkers has led the charge against misinformation. Founded in 1994, Snopes began as a website dedicated to debunking popular urban legends. Since then, it has taken on the role of verifying popular news stories that spread on social media and across fake news sites. Editors of Snopes will fact-check everything from a picture that looks overly photoshopped to poorly worded headlines to full fake news stories, and then explain the facts. They also explain where the fake news originated and if the stories contained any factual elements that may have led to confusion. Thanks to Snopes, hundreds of fake news stories have been fact-checked, and real news has been spread.[3]

hate between people to influence society or politics. Others want to make money off of their fake news by driving people to their websites and showing them advertisements that help them earn money. Still others create fake news for no reason other than that they can. But no matter why they do it, the result is the same: confusion and distrust of real news.

## The Who, What, When, Where, and Why of Fake News

"Fake news" is often used as a derogatory term for any news story that someone disagrees with. But as you've learned, that's not really what it means. Fake news is a very real problem with a very clear definition. Whenever someone calls real journalism "fake news" because they disagree with it or don't like the facts presented, they're making it harder for readers to know what news is real and trustworthy and what is fake or propaganda.[4]

The current problem of fake news rose greatly during the 2016 United States presidential election. Stories that appealed to one political party or the other began appearing online in great quantities, and they were shared by websites that seemed like sources of real news. They came from websites with reputable-sounding names and were shared by people whom others thought they could trust.[5]

One of the biggest fake news story of the modern era was called #pizzagate. The story claimed that Hillary Clinton, the Democratic nominee for president in 2016, helped run a sex

People left signs and flowers outside Comet Ping Pong after a man showed up at the restaurant with a gun, believing a fake news story about crimes taking place there.

trafficking ring located in the basement of a popular pizza parlor in Washington, DC. The story spread like wildfire, and people all over the world believed it, even though it probably sounds crazy to you now. The story was so believable, though, that a man even showed up at the pizza restaurant with a gun looking to free the children he believed were being held by Clinton and her colleagues in the basement.[6]

Reading this story today, you might think that fake news story is an obvious lie. How could anyone believe that? But because of the fiery rhetoric that accompanies elections and the partisan divide that was being felt across the country, people who would otherwise have been suspicious of such a story were compelled to believe it.

Other popular fake news stories also centered on the presidential election. There were stories about Pope Francis, the leader of the worldwide Catholic Church, endorsing Donald Trump for the presidency and about Hillary Clinton endorsing Trump—even though she was running against him at the time.

What made such unbelievable stories seem so plausible? They were shared by multiple fake news outlets, so searching for the story meant readers who were questioning the validity would find a second source to back it up. It might have been the exact same story shared elsewhere, but for a casual newsreader, that was enough to prove it was true. Fake news stories were also shared widely on Twitter and Facebook. When people see stories on social media shared by someone they know or trust, like a friend or a respected adult, they're more likely to believe the story is factual. So while people may have questioned the truth behind some of 2016's biggest lies, once they saw their aunt or cousin or best friend posting the story on social media, they were inclined to believe it was true.

# The Virus Spreads

**F**ake news is able to cause problems in society because of social media. Thanks to the technology that allows us to keep in touch with our friends around the world, see live video from the International Space Station, and find the words to our favorite songs from a small device in our pockets, people can also spread fake news.

## The Social Media Problem

The majority of fake news is spread through social media. The apps and platforms that let you talk to your friends or see what your favorite actors are doing make it easy for anyone who wants to share information to do so. And postings on social media can spread far and wide in no time at all.[1]

When you log on to Facebook or Twitter, you can scroll endlessly through posts from millions of people around the world. Some may be your friends and family or celebrities with familiar names, but many more are strangers. Anyone in the

It's easy to spread fake news through social media because the platforms allow anyone to create an account and post most anything they want, whether it's true or not.

world can create an account on these platforms—or they can create many profiles if they want to spread their message even further.

It's also easy to share content on social media. Most websites allow you to click a button at the top of a story to share it immediately to any one of your social media profiles. You can open a website, click one button, and see a story you've just read spread to your friends, your family, and all your followers.

Sharing information so easily sounds like a good thing, but it means that people don't always know what they're sharing.[2]

Think about the last link you shared on Twitter, or maybe the last news post you liked on Instagram. Did you read the entire article that link led you to, or did you share it based solely on the headline? If you're like 60 percent of the population, you simply shared it. You posted it on Facebook or retweeted it and you didn't think about it again. But by not reading the article, you have no idea what you really shared. The link you shared may have looked legit, but there's a chance it was fake news. Without knowing the content of the article, there's no way to know what you really shared.

Fake news works so well on social media because the creators buy website addresses that sound like real news outlets. There are fake news websites designed to look like CBS News, CNN, the *Guardian*, and even your local newspaper. If you only look at the URL—the website address that you click to get to the article—you are unlikely to know if what you're sharing is real news or fake. Even clicking on the link and opening the page isn't enough to be certain of the quality of the information. To really know what you're sharing, you have to read the entire article.

How did fake news become some of the most-shared content on social media? In a way, it started there. Fake news couldn't exist in the twenty-first century without the help of social media allowing it to spread.

Think about all the websites you visit on a regular basis. Other than checking your email, going to social media

Many people who get their news from social media read only the headlines before sharing the stories themselves, never knowing if the articles are based on facts or not.

websites, or visiting Wikipedia, you probably get the majority of your information by searching for it online through a search engine like Google or Yahoo!. Now, say you want to find out something about Justin Bieber. You could go to his Twitter account, check his Instagram, or look on Wikipedia, but what if it's something new? What if you hear he's releasing a secret album, or maybe he's single again. How would you find out? You would search "Justin Bieber." But if you look up Justin Bieber on Google, you'll find more than 202 million possible web pages to go through.

If you find more than two hundred million pages of information, you're not going to have time to read them all to find the true answer to your question. But you might be able to search on Twitter or Facebook to see what other people are saying. When that happens, you'll see people sharing their opinions and thoughts, but you'll also find a lot of people sharing links—links that have been liked and shared by other people, too.

When someone shares a link, it's like they're saying, "I approved this story." They may not have the authority to do

## The Social Media Cold War

Russia and the United States have long been enemies, from the Cold War of the 1980s and 1990s to the Syrian civil war in which the United States and Russia supported opposite sides. But the latest fight between the United States and Russia is happening online, with Russian bots—or fake accounts programmed to post only specific content—meddling in US elections. During the 2016 presidential election in the United States, Russia used bots on Facebook and Twitter to spread fake news about Hillary Clinton in an effort to convince the American public to vote for Donald Trump. But the bots did not stop after the election. They have continued in the years since to spread fake news and propaganda across social media platforms in an effort to make Americans distrust the news media and each other. Russia believes that by doing this, it will win the current cold war.[3]

Looking up information online seems like a great way to get news, but with so many possible sources, it's not easy to tell from a simple search result if you've found a quality source.

that or have even read the story themselves, but sharing a link comes across as supporting the post it links to. So if you see your best friend share a link saying that Justin Bieber is running for Congress or that he's actually forty years old, you're more likely to give it a click, even if it sounds silly or absurd. You might even see a story your friend shared and read only the headline that shows up on the social media post because you assume that your friend read it and found it credible.

Once you find what you assume is the answer to your question about Justin Bieber, you're probably going to want to share it with your friends. That means you'll likely open the link and then click on one or more of the social media sharing buttons allowing it to post the link directly to your timeline. And that's what fake news creators need.

For a fake news story to be useful to its creators, it needs to do at least one of two things: spread their chosen information or earn them money. When you open a link, you're probably seeing an ad or two on the page, and that helps the original poster earn money, a few pennies at a time. When you share the link, you're both spreading the false information that the creator wants people to read and making sure other people open the link and see those same ads, earning the creator even more money.

If the fake news creators had to rely on you finding their stories via search engines, the chances that a fake story would spread would be slim. Remember how many Justin Bieber results came up when we Googled him? More than two hundred million. If that was the only way to get fake news, you'd rarely find it, and if you did, it would be easy to ignore because no one you know would have found the same story. But with social media, bots and fake news creators can share their false stories and get them seen by thousands or even millions of people almost instantly. And if even 1 percent of those people share the article, it spreads even further.

That chain, from first sharer to final reader, could go on almost infinitely. By the time you read a fake news story, whether it's about Justin Bieber or President Donald Trump, chances are thousands of people have read the story before you, believed it, and shared it with someone else.

## Writing Our Fake History

Now, you might be wondering, "Who actually produces fake news?" Well, there are a lot of people. Some fake news creators are individuals who want to see what they can get away with, but more and more, the fake news creators are people who want to lie to you for profit.

Some of the most prolific fake news creators come from a small town in Macedonia, a country in southeastern Europe.[4] There, young people not much older than you work to build websites and write fake news stories in order to earn a living. Some of them worked on spreading fake news during the 2016 election, and they're already working on creating fake news sites to help spread false information for the 2020 US presidential election.

Why would these young adults halfway around the world want to fool you by spreading fake news? The money. As we discussed earlier, fake news websites can earn their creators money by sharing advertisements with whoever visits their site. Even if an ad earns only a penny per view, that ad could be seen by millions of people each time a fake news story is

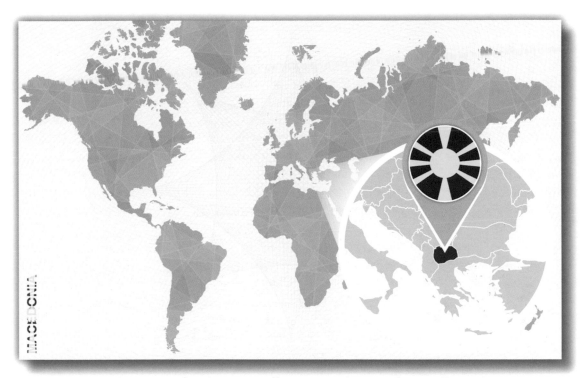

Teenagers in Macedonia, a small country in southeast Europe, published fake news targeting US citizens as a way to earn money.

shared, and if a website shares a lot of fake stories, it will have even more people clicking its links. Some young Macedonians have said they can earn as much as $2,500 a week by creating fake news. That adds up to $130,000 per year—much more than a young person would earn anywhere, let alone in a poor country like Macedonia.

However, young people creating fake news means that other young people—people like you—also have the ability to tell real news from fake. We'll discuss how you can beat your Macedonian counterparts in the next chapter.

# 3

## Fact or Fake News?

**W**ith fake news spreading so easily across the internet, it probably sounds like it's impossible to protect yourself. But it's actually much easier than you think to figure out if you're getting your information from a trustworthy source.

## A Tangled Web of News

There are a bunch of really easy things to look for when you're trying to determine if a story is real or fake, and the first one is the simplest: the URL. The URL is the link you click on to get to an article. It could be something as familiar as http://CNN .com, or it might be something far more complex. Regardless of how long the URL is, there are things you can look for to tell if it's a trustworthy website.

## Check That URL

First, you should look at the part before the ".com." If it's something like CNN or CBS or NYTimes, something you recognize as being a news source, you're off to a good start. You can even delete the rest of the URL after the ".com" to see the homepage of the site, which will help you determine if the website is from a legitimate news publisher. For example, while CNN.com is a real and trusted news source, Breaking-CNN.com is a fake news site responsible for spreading hoaxes.[1]

If that first part of the web address seems safe, check out the ".com." Most news websites use ".com," but some may use ".org" or even ".net." Websites registered in other countries may use a different code. For example, British websites use ".co.uk," while websites based in New Zealand use ".co.nz." If a web address has something after that first period that you're not familiar with or that seems strange, you'll want to double-check your source. So while ABCnews.com is real, ABCnews.com.co (now shut down) was a fake news site that copied the look and feel of the real ABC News website.[2]

Assuming you've gotten this far and the URL appears to point to a real news source, the next thing to do is click the link and visit the site. Once you're on the website, you'll want to look at the full site and check for more signals of authenticity.

## Byline Basics

When you're looking at the article in question, you should look for an author name and a publication date. A publication date is a signal of timeliness. Real news sites make it easy to see when a story was first put online so readers know if the information is new and newsworthy. An author byline is a sign that someone stands behind the story. If you read a story that seems questionable, you should look up the author online. A good journalist will be searchable. They will probably have a public Twitter account or other stories that they've written that you can find. If you can't find anything from a journalist except for bylines on the site you're reading, it's not a great sign,

Some news outlets, like CNN or the *New York Times*, are agreed upon by almost everyone to be quality sources of fact-based information.

but it doesn't always mean something is fake news either. It is, however, a sign that you need to keep checking to verify you've found a quality source.

## What About the "About" Page?

Look at the website's About page. Any reputable news website will have a page explaining what the company is and how to contact its main office. Sometimes this page will be hard to find, but it will usually be linked at the very bottom of the screen.

When you find an About page, you'll be able to read some background on the company and also find a main email or phone number for the office that runs the site. If a website doesn't have an About page, there's a good chance it's not a trustworthy website.

## Satire Versus Fake News

An About page can also be helpful if you've stumbled upon a satirical news website, which is a website that looks like real news but is filled with made-up stories. This is not actually fake news. What's the difference? Fake news pretends to be true, while satirical websites will tell you their stories are make believe, even if they design them to look real. An example of a satirical news source is the *Onion*. The *Onion* looks like a real news website, and some of its headlines sound just like what you would read on *BuzzFeed News* or the *Washington Post*, but they're fake. A site like the *Onion* will admit on its About page that it's publishing satire, and if you search online, you'll find multiple places where the site's humor is explained.

## Reading Between the Lines

Once you've checked out the basic elements of the website you're getting your news from, it's time to dig deeper by reading the article. There are a number of elements that make up a quality news source, and you'll only be able to determine if a story meets those criteria by reading it. Let's examine the criteria of real news.

### Check the Source

First, a trustworthy news article will cite its sources, whether that means quoting people who spoke to the author for the story or linking to other sources they pulled information from, like scientific studies, other news outlets, or press releases. If a story is based only on one source, or worse, doesn't name any sources, there's a good chance the information cannot be confirmed and may be made up.

### Can I Quote You?

You should also question any quotes or bits of information that seem too good or too crazy to be true. If a story quotes a public figure saying something outrageous, there's very little chance that outlet is the only one that got that quote, so you should look it up. Now, we talked about how online searches aren't always reliable, but if you're looking for a very specific bit of information, it's a good way to see if anyone else has published it. Of course, if you find the same quote or tidbit in another news article, you'll have to go through all the steps we've already discussed to determine if that source can be trusted, but it's worth it to make sure you're only believing real news.[3]

Websites like the *Onion* may look like fake news, but they're really satire. They make up all their stories, but they don't try to fool people into believing their news is real.

## Like Your (Writing) Style

You should also look at how the story is written. Does the author talk about himself or herself? Does the journalist tell you their opinion? Quality, professional journalists will almost never mention themselves in a story and will certainly not state their personal opinion. That's because real news is supposed to be unbiased, be honest, and contain only facts. Any opinion in a news story should come from important people being quoted, not from the journalist writing the story.

# Fact-Checking the News

Sometimes you have to do your own digging to get to the bottom of a story, but for a lot of popular news, especially about important issues like politics and the government, there are fact-checking websites like FactCheck.org and Politifact .com that will do the work for you. These fact-checking outlets work by having professional editors and journalists review news stories that contain questionable information and then do additional research and reporting until they get to the truth. Sometimes the fact-check is because a news source was biased or misstated a fact, and other times the quotes in the story are being fact-checked. Presidents and politicians are often the subjects of such fact-checks because they are more likely to misstate the truth in order to appear favorable to voters. In those instances, the fact-checkers are looking at not the work of the reporters, but the truth of the sources they're quoting.

President Donald Trump is famous for calling any news outlet that criticizes him "fake news," including respected publishers like the *Washington Post* and *Time* magazine.

Journalists are also sure to be transparent in their stories. They'll tell you who they talked to, what they saw, and what information they could not obtain. If an article is missing information that would be important to know to understand the importance of the story, or if there are connections made that seem crazy, it's another sign that what you're reading isn't quality news.

It may sound like there's a lot of work you have to do to be able to read even one news article, but most of the time you'll figure out your source's quality quickly, usually within the first few steps. If you have to do more to verify your source, it doesn't mean you're bad at judging the news either—it just means that you care enough to make sure you're only ingesting real, quality news.

# Stopping the Spread

So now you know how to tell if the news you're reading and sharing is real. But what should you do when you see fake news spreading across your social media channels? Just because you're not being fooled anymore doesn't mean your job is over.

If you see someone you know sharing a fake news article, you should point it out. Tweet them, comment on their Facebook post, or send them a Snap explaining that you've done your research and discovered that the story they posted online isn't real. Sometimes your friends will be mad at you for calling them out publicly and they might not believe you, but if you explain that you've found something fake, you're alerting not only your friend but anyone else they might have shared the story with.

Fake news isn't going to stop spreading online just because we know how to find real news. Part of the reason is that

It's important to help your friends and family spot fake news. If someone you know shares a false story, let them know and help them find some real facts worth sharing.

too many people see fake news and don't call it out. It's important to talk to the people in your life about the news and discuss with them what you know about weeding out fake news. This way you can all get your information from the most trustworthy sources.

## Social Media Sharers, Beware!

Avoiding fake news doesn't stop just because you've gotten better at spotting the garbage once you click a link. You also need to be aware of what you do when you're posting online and when you're following others.

When you see a post on social media, no matter who posted it, if there's a link, you need to click it before you share the post. People can unintentionally share the wrong link when they post on social media, or they could be reposting someone else's post that they didn't click through first. By clicking on the link before you share something, you're making an effort to see what it is you're telling your friends and followers to read. You're protecting yourself and your followers not only from fake news but also from mistaken news. For instance, you might have accidentally copied a link to a website you were using to look up information for a homework assignment and then tried to tweet about a great new movie you streamed. If you don't pay attention, you could accidentally tweet your homework while commenting on a movie, creating confusion among the people who read your tweet. The same thing can happen when you're posting about a news article, so always double-check the links before you post them.

You should also pay attention to whom you follow online. Most people don't intentionally share fake news, but if someone you're following continuously shares misinformation, you might want to consider unfollowing them. It's easier to avoid falling for fake news stories if you can avoid reading them at all.

When it comes to what you share, be careful about the headlines you choose to put on your timeline. Sometimes, a real news story could have a headline that sounds like clickbait—something designed to make people click on the link but that has very little to do with the true story. If you're sharing an article with a clickbait-style headline, you should write your own tweet before sharing the link so that you aren't inadvertently giving people the wrong idea about what the article says.

## Follow the News Leaders

Another way to avoid sharing or even encountering fake news on social media is to follow legitimate news sources and professional journalists. These sources will help fill your timelines with quality news so that you'll have real information to turn to when you hear a rumor or see a fake news article that catches your attention.

Across social media, there are signals about which sources can be trusted. Instagram, Twitter, and Facebook all use blue checkmarks to signify that a profile belongs to the person or company it claims to be and that the account is of public interest. Now, a blue checkmark doesn't automatically mean a source is trustworthy, but it's a good start. Look for your local newspaper or TV news station on social media and follow it and some of its journalists, and then see whom those people post about. Reliable sources will do their best to share posts only from other trustworthy sources, so they're a good place to start.

You should also follow some journalists from outlets you know and trust and see what they talk about online. Journalists use social media to share their stories and to discuss other news, and following them will let you see how professional reporters talk about the news. If journalists are on social media questioning a fact or a story, that's a sign that

## Blocking the Bots

Now that you're ready to spot the fake news story and tell others when they're spreading false information, you may wonder to yourself, "Am I the only one doing anything to stop the spread of fake news?" It sure can seem that way when you have to do so much as a news consumer to make sure you have a healthy news diet. But social media platforms are working to rid their sites of fake news, too, and that starts with blocking the bots that spread that news. Facebook removed more than a billion fake accounts from its website in the first six months of 2018, many of which were responsible for sharing fake news or buying ads to promote fake stories.[1] Twitter, meanwhile, suspended more than seventy million bots in May and June 2018 and planned to remove more.[2] By deleting the bot accounts, the social media giants are making it harder for fake news creators to spread their stories and making it safer for you to browse social media without coming across nearly as many false articles.

something is suspicious. If it's a story you're interested in, you can follow the conversation to see why they find the story not worth trusting.

You can also use social media to talk to the people reporting the news. Many journalists are regular users of social media, especially Twitter, and will engage with readers online. If you read a story and you find something a journalist wrote even a little bit questionable, you can go directly to the reporter and

Always read the full story before sharing a link on social media. Facebook should be fun and informative, not full of fake news.

ask them to clarify what they wrote. You can even tweet the public figures quoted in most stories to ask them about what was written about them.

When you're online, having fun using social media, it may be hard to think about whether you're reading real news. But the same platforms that allow you to share your life with your friends and family also allow fake news creators to use you to spread their stories. It's easy to fall for their posts, too. They are designed to look and read like real news stories to fool even smart, informed readers like you.

Fake news creators depend on people clicking "Share" on their stories without ever reading, and they hope that you'll be uninformed enough to fall for even their most outrageous headlines on Twitter or Facebook. That's why, even when you feel confident that you can tell real news from junk on first glance, it's important to remember all the tips you've learned so that you never fall prey to a particularly well-disguised piece of fake news.

When fake news has the chance to spread widely, it can disrupt not only your information stream but our greater social and political structures.

It's only by remaining alert and constantly checking your sources that you'll be able to avoid fake news on social media and become part of the solution instead of an inadvertent part of the problem. By helping to prevent the spread of fake news, you're helping to keep democracy and society intact.

# Chapter Notes

## Chapter 1: What Is Fake News?

1. "The Great Moon Hoax," History.com, https://www.history.com/this-day-in-history/the-great-moon-hoax.
2. Laura Sydell, "We Tracked Down a Fake-News Creator in the Suburbs. Here's What We Learned," NPR.com, November 23, 2016, https://www.npr.org/sections/alltechconsidered/2016/11/23/503146770/npr-finds-the-head-of-a-covert-fake-news-operation-in-the-suburbs.
3. "About Us," Snopes.com, https://www.snopes.com/about-snopes.
4. Jennifer Peters, "Fake News Remains Top Industry Concern in 2017," News Media Alliance, October 4, 2017, https://www.newsmediaalliance.org/fake-news-concern.
5. Hannah Ritchie, "Read All About It: The Fakest News Stories of 2016," CNBC.com, December 30, 2016, https://www.cnbc.com/2016/12/30/read-all-about-it-the-biggest-fake-news-stories-of-2016.html.
6. Faiz Siddiqui and Susan Svrluga, "N.C. man Told Police He Went to D.C. Pizzeria with Gun to Investigate Conspiracy Theory," *Washington Post*, December 5, 2016, https://www.washingtonpost.com/news/local/wp/2016/12/04/d-c-police-respond-to-report-of-a-man-with-a-gun-at-comet-ping-pong-restaurant/?utm_term=.2417fdcc5456.

## Chapter 2: The Virus Spreads

1. Paul Chadwick, "Why Fake News on Social Media Travels Faster Than the Truth," *Guardian*, March 19, 2018, https://www

.theguardian.com/commentisfree/2018/mar/19/fake-news-social-media-twitter-mit-journalism.

2. Caitlin Dewey, "6 in 10 of You Will Share This Link Without Reading It, a New, Depressing Study Says," *Washington Post*, June 16, 2016, https://www.washingtonpost.com/news/the-intersect/wp/2016/06/16/six-in-10-of-you-will-share-this-link-without-reading-it-according-to-a-new-and-depressing-study/?utm_term=.d2736b0dc86b.

3. Jon Swaine, "Twitter Admits Far More Russian Bots Posted on Election Than It Had Disclosed," *Guardian*, January 19, 2018, https://www.theguardian.com/technology/2018/jan/19/twitter-admits-far-more-russian-bots-posted-on-election-than-it-had-disclosed.

4. Florence Davey-Attlee and Isa Soares, "The Fake News Machine: Inside a Town Gearing Up for 2020," CNN.com, https://money.cnn.com/interactive/media/the-macedonia-story.

## Chapter 3: Fact or Fake News?

1. Jon Swaine, "Twitter Admits Far More Russian Bots Posted on Election Than It Had Disclosed," *Guardian*, January 19, 2018, https://www.theguardian.com/technology/2018/jan/19/twitter-admits-far-more-russian-bots-posted-on-election-than-it-had-disclosed.

2. Jack Murtha, "How Fake News Sites Frequently Trick Big-Time Journalists," *Columbia Journalism Review*, May 26, 2016, https://www.cjr.org/analysis/how_fake_news_sites_frequently_trick_big-time_journalists.php.

3. "Breaking News Consumer's Handbook: Fake News Edition," WNYC, November 18, 2016, https://www.wnyc.org/story/breaking-news-consumer-handbook-fake-news-edition.

## Chapter 4: Stopping the Spread

1. Kurt Wagner and Roni Molla, "Facebook Has Disabled Almost 1.3 Billion Fake Accounts Over the Past Six Months," Recode, May 15, 2018, https://www.recode.net/2018/5/15/17349790/facebook-mark-zuckerberg-fake-accounts-content-policy-update.
2. Craig Timberg and Elizabeth Dwoskin, "Twitter Is Sweeping Out Fake Accounts Like Never Before, Putting User Growth at Risk," *Washington Post*, July 6, 2018, https://www.washingtonpost.com/technology/2018/07/06/twitter-is-sweeping-out-fake-accounts-like-never-before-putting-user-growth-risk/?utm_term=.a0a1663b30b9.

# Glossary

**app**  A software program that allows you to access a social media platform or website from your smartphone.

**bad actor**  A person or persons who are behaving in a way they know to be bad. Fake news creators are bad actors.

**bot**  A fake social media account, typically run by a computer code and not a person, that posts only very specific content. Fake news is spread through the use of bots that target users tweeting about certain topics.

**Facebook**  The largest social media platform in the world, Facebook allows people and businesses to connect and share content. Facebook is also responsible for allowing fake news to spread around the globe.

**fake news**  Any story that is not factual and is written to purposely fool people and spread false information. For a story to be fake news, it must not only spread misinformation, but it must do so with knowledge that the information is inaccurate.

**hoax**  A prank designed to fool people into believing a fake news story is real.

**platform**  A website that allows people to post their own content and share it on that website. Social media websites, such as Facebook and Twitter, are known as platforms.

**satire**  A made-up story that is written in a way that makes fun of real news and can often look like real news. Although satirical stories are fake, they are not the same as fake news.

**search engine**  Any website that allows you to search for information across a wide range of sources. Google, Yahoo!, and Bing are some of the most popular search engines.

**social media**  Any website or platform that allows people to share information and links with other users in a public fashion. Facebook, Twitter, and Reddit are some of the most popular social media platforms.

**Twitter**  A social media platform that allows users to post short messages and share them with a public audience.

**URL**  A website address. "URL" stands for "uniform resource locator" and is the string of code you type in to access a particular page on the internet. For example, Facebook.com is the URL for Facebook.

# Further Reading

## Books

Dell, Pamela. *Understanding the News*. North Mankato, MN: Capstone Press, 2018.

Krieger, Emily. *Real or Fake? 3*. Washington, DC: National Geographic Children's Books, 2018.

Share, Jeff. *Media Literacy Is Elementary: Teaching Youth to Critically Read and Create Media*. New York, NY: Peter Lang, 2015.

Young, Kevin. *Bunk: The Rise of Hoaxes, Humbug, Plagiarists, Phonies, Post-Facts, and Fake News*. Minneapolis, MN: Graywolf Press, 2017.

## Websites

### NewseumED

*www.newseumed.org*

The Newseum, the national journalism museum in Washington, DC, offers resources for learning media literacy on its education-focused website. Among the offerings available are lesson plans and easy tips and tricks for spotting fake news, such as the "Fact Finder" guide to media literacy.

Facebook and Twitter: @NewseumED

## The News Literacy Project

*www.newslit.org*

A national nonprofit focused on fact-checking and news literacy, the News Literacy Project offers resources for students who want to know if the news they're consuming is real and trustworthy.

Facebook: @TheNewsLiteracyProject

Twitter: @NewsLitProject

## Snopes

*www.snopes.com*

Snopes is a fun and easy-to-use resource for fact-checking even the most outlandish stories you come across online. While it debunks dozens of fake news stories each week (and points out surprising true stories that appear fake), it also offers a comprehensive "Field Guide to Fake News" so you can learn how to fact-check the stories on your own.

Facebook and Twitter: @snopes

# Index